DIAL
WITH THE STARS

AND

HYMN TO LIGHT

HENRYK SKOLIMOWSKI

DIALOGUES WITH THE STARS

AND

HYMN TO LIGHT

HENRYK SKOLIMOWSKI

DETROIT
CREATIVE FIRE PRESS
2015

All rights reserved. Creative Fire Press is a division of *The Walden Group*, a Michigan non-profit educational corporation.

Production manager: David Skrbina.

Library of Congress Cataloging-in-Publication Data

Skolimowski, Henryk
Dialogues with the Stars

        p.   cm.
Includes bibliographical references.

ISBN 978-1511559560 (pbk.: alk. paper)
1. Philosophy.
2015

Printing number: 9 8 7 6 5 4 3 2 1

Printed in the United States of America on acid-free paper.

PREFACE   7

1ST DIALOGUE   9

2ND DIALOGUE   13

3RD DIALOGUE   19

4TH DIALOGUE   25

5TH DIALOGUE   33

6TH DIALOGUE   39

7TH DIALOGUE   47

8TH DIALOGUE   55

9TH DIALOGUE   61

10TH DIALOGUE   67

EPILOGUE:
HOW HAVE I LEARNT TO DIALOGUE WITH THE STARS?   71

HYMN TO LIGHT   77

DIALOGUES WITH THE STARS

AND

HYMN TO LIGHT

HENRYK SKOLIMOWSKI

PREFACE

Can you dialogue with the stars…and remain sane? Yes you can. I have had a good fortune to do so. This is rare. But not entirely startling. Let us remember: We all come from the stellar dust. Some fragments of my stellar existence have been residing in my being from the time immemorial. Permit me to repeat, we are all fragments of the stellar universe.

I have been fortunate enough to play in my imagination with my stellar beginnings. Moreover, my dialogues with the stars may be seen as dialogues of stars themselves — yes, when they acquired human consciousness. Alternatively, you may see these dialogues as dialogues with myself — when I was inspired by the presence of stars just over my head.

There is more to us than bones and lots of blood. Some deeper layers are hidden in you. They can be reached if you have enough courage and imagination to uncover them. You will find from my dialogues that it is possible to tune to the consciousness of the stars — if you have perseverance and courage to do so.

If you find that the stars are not responding, don't worry. There may be another time. Stars are very patient. They are always ready for a dialogue, if you summon enough courage and determination. Courage is required for things extraordinary. One of them is dialoguing with the stars.

What follows are dialogues with the star Annabel. What I am presenting in these dialogues is a cosmic play in some ten short acts. Some readers will find them fictitious. And I will not be offended. All dramas and good plays are fictitious. Actually all significant cosmic knowledge is fictitious. And the pretentious science, which attempts to describe it, is fictitious itself.

I do not expect the readers to believe in the truths, which Annabel and my humble self have tried to convey. I expect the readers to enjoy the dialogues as a form of theatre. If you are taken to a significant art exhibition, there is no guarantee that you will experience a great thrill. But it is a good idea to come with an open mind so that you can experience something unusual.

The play, of which my dialogues are composed, is about the stars. But there is something important in the background. It is the CANVAS. I am inviting you to the most magnificent canvas that has ever existed. And the stars are the greatest actors that ever existed or will exist. At times we have the glimpses of it. But most of the time we are numb and unseeing—while the greatest play ever staged and performed happens in front of our eyes.

Whoever is awoken to the glories of the Theatre of the Stars is truly privileged to live in the universe of radiant stars, which lend some of their radiance to us. That is what my Dialogues wanted to convey and to share.

THE
1ST DIALOGUE
WITH THE STAR
ANNABEL

At the point where the Milky Way almost touches the Vega constellation, there is a big triangle of stars. Within it the intensity of the stars of the Milky Way is perhaps the most intense. Also within this triangle there is a moderately bright star, which I have named Annabel. I have had several conversations with this star. I noticed that the stars are unusually radiant tonight. I spread a thick canvas on the ground, among the pines, and watched them. After quite a while, I tentatively started a dialogue... with the star I named Annabel.

H. Any message...?

A. What message?

H. From you...

A. What kind of message do you want?

H. A nice message.

A. You have it...nice messages are easy.

H. Well, I meant a deep message.

A. For this you need to wait a little.

H. I really meant a profound one.

A. That would take quite a lot of time.

H. Are you so slow?

A. No, you are so slow...to receive it.

H. I see...

A. Yes...but you see so dimly and rarely.

H. What about the ultimate message?

A. Perhaps for this one you would have to wait until your next life.

H. Is that so?

A. Unless you get it...from yourself...in this lifetime.

A long silence.

H. What about this ultimate message?

11

A. Just think of it...

H. I know! I know! It must be so simple that it is almost unbelievable.

A. Correct!

H. Yes, I have it!

A. What is it?

H. *BE*.

A. You have got it.

I sighed with relief and looking around me I thought to myself: yes, I have all stars as my friends — what an immense feeling!

The stars are always there — immovable and yet moveable. They are peaceful, patient and radiant. They are always kind and benign. They never bark at you like dogs and people. They are our friends. The more time you spend among them, the easier it is to live among human beings.

THE
2ND DIALOGUE

I went to the mountains some nights later. I sat for a while and tentatively started the dialogue again.

H. What am I supposed to do?

Long silence, no response. Finally in a muted way I hear:

A. Whatever you do will be ok.

I don't like this response so I say:

H. Even if I do nothing?

Yes.

Even if I do little?

Yes.

Even if I do a lot?

Yes.

Even if I do a tremendous lot?

Yes.

I am perplexed by this time. And try to derive a conclusion.

H. So nothing and a tremendous lot have the same value?

A. (Hesitatingly) Yes.

It cannot be.

It can in our universe… We do not use any of your evaluating terms…

But you must have some kind of logic to judge things.

No, we don't.

How is it possible? *(I say this a bit irritated)*

It is *(and she says it with a certain finality)*.

How is it possible… with all these eons of time you have existed?

What eons of time?

Well, the universe will be 25 billion years old before it runs its course.

The phrase "25 billion years" or even "one year" mean nothing to us.

15

I am flabbergasted and impatient.

H. What has meaning to you?

Long silence, and then…

A. You don't understand. For us—not bounded by time—one second and 25 billion years is all the same. For us the whole history of the universe—as you call it—is just one flair up. It takes no time, because there is no time.

H. *(to himself)* I am beginning to understand. But it is so strange to live in the universe without logic, without significance, without time and duration.

A. It is so only for you, human beings, who must have logic, who must evaluate things, who must have all these dramas…

Dramas? What dramas?

You have invented time, and your consciousness is oppressed by time because you live in fear—in the fear of mortality. You are afraid of death, which is a creation of your consciousness, which has given rise to uncertainty, despair and longing for immortality—another of your chimera. All of this creates these superfluous dramas in your universe.

I see, I see….

And I fell in a deep coma of meditation. After a long silence, while still lying on the ground on a thick canvas, I pleadingly turn to Annabel and I say, really to myself:

H. You and other stars with which I have talked always urged me to transcend, and transcend and transcend—transcend all limits of knowledge and of human understanding. What is the use?

A. *(unexpectedly returns to the conversation)* What do you mean? What do you want to tell me—in your mournful way?

H. What is the use of having all these insights about time, and about the human dramas—caused by the fears of mortality—if I cannot share them?

You may try to share them.

You are very naïve. I can hardly share with ordinary people more refined knowledge, which is already accepted by more spiritual people and seers. How will I share these new insights, which are beyond everything that is known and accepted? Yes, with whom will I share them and how?

After a long silence Annabel finally responds.

16

You will share them with yourself. You will not need to share these insights with anybody. You will be like God. Gods do not need to share their illuminations with others.

Perhaps they do, after all...

(Laughs and says:) Have it your way.

I again fall into deep coma and mutter to myself: talking to the stars is a strange and dangerous business. Yet, I also derive an important conclusion from this dialogue with Annabel, which was as follows: For the limitless imagination, there are no boundaries; and there are no things impossible. This conclusion thrills me and frightens me at the same time.

Then I folded my canvas and returned from the mountain valley back to the village. While on the dirt road, I once again looked at the Milky Way, smiled joyously, seeing its myriads of lights—and asked:

What do I owe you?

The Milky Way responded: Everything.

I asked another question: And what do you owe me?

The Milky Way responded: Everything.

THE
3RD DIALOGUE

Once more I traveled to the stars.
And submerged myself in their
immensity and radiance.
Inadvertently I turned to Annabel
and almost casually said:

H. Are you still there...?

She smiled back but a bit jeeringly.
This jeering smile unhinged me a
little. I turned away from her to
other vast spaces. I went in my mind
through these colossal changes from
the cosmic dust to the radiant
galaxies. Then to the beginning of
the groping life... Then I observed
life unfolding and flourishing. Then
I watched with amazement the birth
of the sky gods—their brilliance and
sense of transcendence. Then I
observed how these sky gods
constituted themselves into
organized religions. It appears
Annabel was watching my mind.

A. So you are trying to figure it
out, all of it. What has happened
and why it happened.

I was jolted out of my contemplative
reveries—partly annoyed and partly
delighted. I said:

H. Yes, I am. Do I have any other
choice?

A. You could have another choice
if you were not so stubborn.

Then I would not have been
myself, would I?

So you want to know why these
sky gods, who ultimately created
organized religions, were so
different from the other gods, the
earlier gods.

Yes, I would like to know that. The
earlier gods were earth gods. Well,
more often than not they were
goddesses. They were so much
closer to the earth, so much more
organic, so much woven into the
tapestry of the biological life
surrounding the humans. These
early deities of the Matriarchal
period were so naturally merging
into the cycles and rhythms of
human life. And then the sudden
arrival of the sky gods, which
disturbed all the natural cycles,
including changing the lunar
calendar.

So, what do you want to know?

Well, to begin with, why did these sky gods descend to earth and overpower us humans? Why are they so far away and so incomprehensible?

Would you rather prefer to continue dwelling in the old caves and worshipping old trees and revere birds as deities?

You are putting me on the spot. Let me look at the situation from a different angle. I know that before the sky gods descended on earth, there were no religious wars; there was no persecution because you didn't worship the right deities. Spiritual life was so easy, although they did not use the term "spiritual life." It was just ordinary life, woven into the rest of the breathing nature.

You are rather romantic with these old fashioned notions.

I don't know that. I don't know whether I would be so unhappy by being at one with nature and all creation. Deep in my soul I feel that I am unhappy by being alienated from nature and all creation. Yes, I feel that the sky gods alienated people from the natural world by constantly demanding allegiance to the new deities, which are so strange to humans.

Are you calling the deities of organized religions unnatural?

I don't know... Perhaps I do. Are they natural? For me the tree is natural and human love is natural. Let me tell you another problem with the sky gods.

What is it?

You see, these sky gods, which descended on the earth, were so powerful, so superior in their understanding—in comparison with the original indigenous people. Why didn't they make a pact among themselves and start to rule wisely for the benefit of all?

They had to act through local people as intermediaries. And these intermediaries were not so bright.

Well, yes. But why didn't they make the local people wise?

Perhaps it was not in their powers to do so.

So these omnipotent sky gods are not so omnipotent and may be not so great as they claim to be.

You don't understand. All gods are limited.

But this is not what we are told by our priests!

What you are told and what is the truth may be two different things.

What is the truth about the sky gods?

A long silence.

H. So you are not responding...

A. You may not be ready for my answers.

H. Let me share with you another problem of mine. The invasion of the sky gods was like a deluge, which flooded the earth. Why have they done it? Why not leave poor humans as they were by letting them worship natural deities with which they were so comfortable? Why did they require indigenous humans to change their biological nature into transcendent beings?

Annabel took a bit of time to respond. After a while I thought that she was unable to give me any answer at all. Then she spoke.

The story is long and complicated, as you are aware. Look at the radiant galaxies. They are so different from the original stardust. Look at the glory of life, which emerged from the original slime. What a difference again! Some 5000-6000 years ago, it was felt in the bowels of the Cosmos that the time had arrived to push evolution to a new level. Hence, the revolution of the sky gods.

And who is doing the pushing, you the stars?

No, no. Light itself. Light is the source from which everything originates, including all the stars and galaxies.

Why would Light want to do all this pushing?

Hmm... how should I put it—for the sake of its own journey. Actually Light is not doing any pushing. It is just unfolding. After it unfolded into ordinary biological life, it decided to go upward and deeper. It started to dream about the human life—as endowed with transcendent and divine attributes.

Why would it want to do that? Are we so important to Light?

You don't understand. It didn't want to do it for you—as ordinary egotistical human beings. It has done so because all human beings are off-springs of Light, are part of the intrinsic process of unfolding Light.

I see... And I don't see... I see... I see! And when I see, I am dumbfounded by what I see.

What do you see?

That all is Light. And we are a part of it. Nothing but Light... But...

But what?

But why do religions tell us otherwise, that at the beginning was God who created light, out of which came the rest of the universe?

I have told you already that even gods are limited and so are religions.

What are you telling me? Say it more clearly.

It is simple, when we see it from our stellar cosmic perspective. It is clearly known among us, the stars, that all religions came from light and are expressions of the power and potency of Light; so it is with gods, of all gods, of all religions.

And then there was a long silence. I emerged from my deep trance, blinked my eyes. What strange things the stars are telling me. Is Annabel confusing me? So perhaps I should not dialogue with her anymore. I ponder over this question for a while. I got up and looked at the Milky Way. The stars were smiling at me radiantly. There was a strange truth emanating from them. So I decided that I should talk to Annabel further. Perhaps she is not confusing me but un-clouding my mind. It is a strange business to talk to the stars. You must be strong to be able to bear their messages.

THE
4TH DIALOGUE

ON THE
CONNECTED UNIVERSE

H. Surrounded by a deep silence, the other night, I have been pondering about the nature of our dialogues.

A. What were you pondering about?

What has actually been going on in our dialogues? You have been so generous with your insights and often so articulate with your ideas.

Let me tell you that you have done quite well. You have been able to follow my ideas and insights.

Kind of you to acknowledge that. But what is the meaning of it all? I know that we all come from the stars. That we and the stars are one. That the whole Cosmos is one essential unity of extraordinary complexity and simplicity—at the same time. I know that it is a strange idea that I can talk to a star... and yet not strange at all. Stranger things than that have been happening in our Cosmos almost daily. But on the level of the human mind: who are you and who am I? Am I your creation? Or are you my creation? I know that

without your stellar inspiration, I could not conceive these far out and intriguing ideas on time, on the soul, and the rest. I am grateful to Light that I could dip into the recesses of your consciousness and could understand your insights about the human condition and myself.

So far so good. What troubles you then?

How shall I put it? I admit that I was created by stars and illumined by them. But what if the other possibility is true: that you are created by me?

So, I am created by you to teach you and instruct you—that which you somehow already know... for otherwise, I could not create you and instruct you in such a way that you could understand so well.

Something of that sort.

Yes, it is an intriguing possibility. But this picture has deeper layers of mystery. How could you create me to instruct you with such luminosity and in such depth unless you had been instructed earlier by some stellar wisdom to project onto me these exciting ideas, which I would later give to you. Do you follow me?

Yes, I do. I think I do.

A clever boy.

Where are we, then, in our discussion on the nature of wisdom, which comes from the stars, while the stars, and all their attributes, are created by the human mind—which creates the stars in a decidedly anthropocentric manner... otherwise we could not have had these lofty conversations on the subjects.

The answer is, of course, deeper than the human mind can conceive—at least at first. We are living in an intelligent Universe. The Cosmos is throbbing with intelligence, mind and spirituality. But these attributes of the Universe are not fixed, static, frozen in their state. On the contrary, they are evolving, unfolding, in the state of becoming and maturing. The whole Cosmos is in the state of becoming, including mind, spirituality, religions and gods... including the awareness of the stars—and what you can learn from them, and what you cannot.

Hold on a little. I don't quite follow this last point. Are you limited in your intelligence, which is also evolving? Or is it us, limited humans, who are evolving and at certain times we can learn less— because we are less evolved, and at other times, we can learn more— when we are more evolved?

It is both. It is one interwoven process. The intelligence of the stars and your own intelligence are connected. When you are more intelligent and luminous, the stars around you are more intelligent and luminous... and can respond to your questions more luminously and beautifully.

Why could your intelligence be connected with our intelligence and somehow be dependent on it?

You still don't understand how deeply and beautifully things are connected in the Universe. I mentioned that the whole Cosmos is in the state of becoming, including Mind. Mind is not an ordinary item of the Cosmos. It is a sort of magnificent glass through which everything is seen in a clear, deep and resplendent way, or through glass darkly — in a murky, blurred, and shallow way. As mind is so the universe is, so your intelligence is, so the level of your conversation is, so your spiritual awareness is.

I am beginning to see... let me continue: as our mind is, so our religions are, so our images of god are, and the attributes that we attribute to gods are, and our relationships with god are.

Yes, you are getting it. It is all an intertwined process of creation of incredible beauty and power. You are not creating it through your mind. Your mind and my stellar intelligence are all parts of the endless creation. You are at best co-creating with the Universe—if you use your mind intelligently and wisely.

Wait a minute. Let me catch my breath. How does my wisdom come into the equation? What if I have none... or very little of it?

Then nothing much happens in your Universe. Your wisdom is part of the general intelligence of the Universe. You cultivate it in order to get along with the Universe, at least the higher reaches of it.

Hmm...This business of wisdom... It is so delicate and at times nebulous. We don't know how to acquire it because it is not taught at schools and universities. Yet, we are supposed to acquire it somehow. How interesting. Another interesting phenomenon of our times is that people talk about the epoch of wisdom, which, according to some, is on the horizon; and according to others will start happening in a millennium or two. Still, other people say that we can intuit this coming epoch of wisdom if we have enough insight in ourselves. How does this talk square with your idea of the unfolding intelligence of the Cosmos.

Well, with patience and perseverance we can explain what people mean by the coming epoch of wisdom. You see, your times are hard and confusing. And people know, almost all of them now, that there is not enough intelligence and wisdom in existing institutions and particular individuals to find lasting solutions to your agonizing problems. Therefore, they project and anticipate the coming epoch of wisdom, which will sort out things in a radical and satisfactory manner.

Is this then wishful thinking, this longing for the epoch of wisdom?

Not at all. Cosmic intelligence is evolving all the time. The brightest human beings use their imagination to envisage the epoch of wisdom and its characteristics. They are subconsciously co-creating this new epoch. Besides, we live in a sensitive and intelligent Universe, which is aware—in one sense or another—what is the situation in the

Cosmos and in the human Universe. The Cosmic intelligence is aware of the suffering of Mother Earth and of the suffering of human beings under the yoke of unreasonable demands of the mechanistic and electronic civilization. And this same intelligence is, in its own way, fashioning the wisdom epoch as an antidote.

What you are saying is very fascinating, but also, a bit nebulous.

Let me explain it in another way. One of your poets, Shelley, once said: "Poets are the gigantic mirrors in which futurity casts its shadow on the present." This is a fantastic insight. It means that exceptional poets and some seers are capable of intuiting what is brewing in deeper layers of the consciousness of evolution—and also express their insights in lucid words. Mind you, these layers of the future epoch of wisdom are not stored there, ready and finished, waiting to be unveiled. No, nothing is there ready, finished, permanent, pre-determined. Everything is in *status nascendi,* in the process of creation. The substance and nature of the wisdom epoch are being forged by your agonies and your genius. As the result of the interaction of your needs for change and your longing for the wisdom epoch with the

larger consciousness outside—there will emerge a new epoch of restoration and renewal; of integration and beauty.

Well, it seems to me that you are saying to us that we, as humans, must be bold, active and imaginative—not stand still until we totally disintegrate.

Absolutely so. Your intelligence is part of the Cosmic intelligence. You must be audacious to weave your best designs of what your future could be into the larger patterns of cosmic consciousness.

If I may continue, we must realize that it is a privilege of intelligent and imaginative minds to be able to talk with stars—and imbibe their stellar wisdom, which is again part of a larger cosmic intelligence.

Right again.

And it would also follow that we should not be too impressed with the closed and sometimes even moronic minds of economists and scientists of the old school, whose minds are closed and cut off from the vital sources of understanding and wisdom. We might suggest at the same time that our rationality should be broad and open to the vast offerings of the Universe. It is entirely rational to take advantage of all resources of knowledge. To be intelligent and enlightened is to open yourself to new resources of imagination and to new wonders of the Universe. After all, Albert Einstein has said himself: "mind without imagination is as good as dead."

Well spoken. You seem to have grasped the design of the Universe well enough. Now you need to act on your knowledge; with wisdom and prudence; but also with courage.

THE
5TH DIALOGUE

ON THE SOUL

H. And what shall we say on the Soul, Annabel?

A. It is a subject better not to be touched.

Why so?

Because the humans have built too many contorted structures about the idea and have become lost in the process.

Hmm… How is it among the stars? Do you have a better idea what the soul may mean?

First of all, we don't need to use the term. But if we had to use something approximate to what you call soul, we would say that: Soul is the *élan vital* of our being, which means radiance, endurance, evolution, the capacity to co-exist with Light, to be nourished by Light and to serve IT, for the glory of all… including things unfathomable, which have not yet come into existence.

It sounds quite interesting, actually. But could we, the humans, not use this idea—you have just

described—for our identification of our sense of the soul?

No, you could not. You are too small for that. You are too tied in your theological and anthropocentric knots… too egocentric—always trying to use the vehicle of the soul for your individual salvation.

It may be just it—what you just said. We are too cramped by our smallness to be able to understand the largeness of the soul.

You have said it well: you cannot be that small and understand the largeness and magnificence of the soul.

Say something more on the subject.

Actually, it is hard to express it in words. Soul is this immensity that you possess, and of which you are most of the time unaware. Soul is this potency which is hiding in you, is this enormous being which is already there, and yet which you still have to actualize. Only very exceptional human beings have actualized this sheer potency to become souls incarnate. And these individuals do not talk about the Soul. They are it!

So most of the theological discussions about the soul are a lot of garbage?

You may say so. But say it softly so that the defenders of the status quo do not hear you. Otherwise you will be in trouble, as you are well aware.

Why is this idea of Soul so attractive to us and so difficult to comprehend?

Well, you want to make soul your personal property, or at best the property which you share with your religion or your church. Soul is not the property of any religion, or any church, or any group of people. It is this Enormous Breath of the Universe, which makes things happen—which ultimately transforms awkward caterpillars into colorful butterflies, ordinary blocks of marble into Aphrodites of Knidos, ordinary humans into exemplary saints.

You are inspired now. Keep going.

What do you want to know?

I don't quite know how to ask it. Well, do tell me why do we need the idea of the soul, we human beings.

Because you must have something larger than you are to guide you. Smallness generates smallness. The idea of the soul is the lamp to remind you what you can become. It is a pointer, which shows the ways you can take. You need a map to guide you and give you directions. The present directions, in your confused secular society, dictated by consumerism and materialism lead you nowhere, so often lead you astray. The present society and its ideologues take you to be much smaller than you are.

Now what about the individual soul in addition to the Cosmic Soul. We seem to be attached to the individual soul.

Yes, you are. And it is at this point that you are getting into trouble.

Why so?

Because your egoistic and small nature reasserts itself. Your soul is not your own soul. It is only a reflection of the Universal Soul, which some call the Universal Mind. Your blood is your own, your heart is your own, but your soul, this is a difficult matter... I don't want to complicate it. But I don't want to oversimplify it.

Just say what it is.

You foolish flying tiger! You think it is that simple? The whole beauty of the human condition and the whole beauty of the unfolding universe is that it is evolving, maturing, becoming. The soul in you belongs to this evolving universe. You possess only a seed of it in yourself. And you need to work on this seed to BECOME. In some, this seed never grows into anything. Unrealized people. In some, this seed develops into a little plant. Half-realized people. In some this seed flowers magnificently. Fully realized people. It is those last people who make us aware what fully ensouled people mean, what spiritual maturity is about. Yes, spiritual maturity is about growing and maturing the human soul. Nobody can do it for you but you yourself. You are your own spiritual gardener, you are the sole maintainer of your soul. You have it and you don't have it. You have it if you cultivate it. But never forget this important truth. This seed in you does not belong to you alone. It belongs to the whole humanity. Nay, it belongs to the whole Cosmos. Because the Cosmos is spiritually so pregnant, it brought forward so many spiritual people and Big Spiritual Lights, which have changed the nature of human society and the nature of the whole Cosmos. Have no fear about the future. Spiritual Light is pervading the Cosmos. This light will be embodied in new spiritual human beings. They will put aright the course of the human universe. It will not be easy but it will done.

Do you mean to say that through spiritual people we shall find right solutions?

Yes, the future belongs to spiritual people. Because only they will be able to survive. I bid you now farewell.

THE
6TH DIALOGUE

ON THE
ETERNAL BLISS

I arrive at my favorite terrace in the fold of the mountains, some distance away from the village. The conditions are perfect. The heavens are ablaze with radiance. The temperature is just right, not too cold, not too humid. I spread my canvas on the ground and situate it so that my head directly faces the big triangle of stars within which Annabel resides. I put on my warm jacket and lay down. Now I am at home, among the stars, almost being touched by them. In my motionless state, absorbed by their iridescent energy, which is showered on me from all the directions, I am completely surrounded by the stars. I cannot remember this kind of experience earlier—to be surrounded by the stars from all directions.

I have read in one of the Tibetan texts that through some yogic exercises, one can directly consume the energy of the stars. In spite of some efforts, I could not find these exercises. Yet in my own way, I feel and know that I am now being nourished by the stars, by their radiance and energy. There is something intoxicating in this spectacle of the stars pouring their energy in the pores of my body and the recesses of my mind. I feel privileged to be able to inhale this great energy. What if this inhalation is just an illusion of my mind? Well, yes, (I smile to myself) I am sorry for those who have brainwashed themselves to think so; and who can never experience the ultimate glory of being enfolded by the cosmic energy.

I have already been lying on the ground for several minutes, gently embracing the stars and being embraced by them. Then a shooting star in the vicinity of the big triangle crosses the skies. It welcomes me. And I know that. The time has arrived for another conversation with Annabel. I have been gazing at her for some time, not knowing how to start. Then I tentatively begin.

H. How is it out there? How are you?

A. It is always the same. And I am always the same.

I don't know what to say next. But I persevere.

H. And how am I?

A. You are always changing. Such is the condition of your earthly existence.

So who is better off? You in your regal permanence, or myself in my fleeting changing state, but amidst freedom and creativity?

The first part of the question is silly. But the second part of the question is interesting. You are imperfect in your continuous change and striving. But you possess freedom and creativity. And what is the price of these is a great question.

Would you prefer to change your state of being with mine?

Another silly question.

I didn't mean to be silly. I only meant to tease you a little.

(*sternly*) The stars are not tease-able.

I was straightened up by this reprimand and thought to myself: well, yes but perhaps they are adorable. Annabel read my thoughts and responded.

A. Perhaps they are adorable, but not in the human sentimental way.

H. How right you are. What would I be in the human world without this immensity of the stars and their energy, which, I know, is reverberating in all my cells and in every atom of my brain. This admiration for the stellar realms is what makes you adorable.

Now you are making sense.

But tell me why you, from the realm of your imperturbable perfection ever bother to talk to us, to take interest in us, and to guide us here and there?

Because we cannot think and articulate the state of our existence in the way you can—consciously and deliberately.

So we are your articulators, heralds of consciousness—of the cosmos, as it unfolds in ever more forceful and deliberate manner.

Something like that. But don't be too conceited and puffed up. You are nothing without us. We are quintessentially part and parcel of your energy and your entire being. We are cosmically one. We have already established this in earlier dialogues. We, the stars, need human consciousness to know where we are and who we are. We

42

need human consciousness to know, consciously, our destiny. This is why we are helping you. And 'helping' is not the right term. More adequate way would be to say this is why we are participating in your project.

Partly because we are participating in *your* project?

Yes!

It is a funny business, these cosmic connections.

Yes, but you should not call it 'funny.' Funny it is not, but wonderful it is.

This is really what I meant—it is wonderful, but opaque and mysterious. I have noticed in our earlier dialogues that you cannot help us in our articulations but you can recognize them, once they have occurred—as a part of your unfolding, so to speak.

Yes, it is something like that. If we could articulate, and express our articulations in some kind of language, we would not have needed you—humans—as our articulators and antennae. We could perhaps even express all these matters more deeply and concisely. But we do not have the power of your articulation.

And you don't have our creativity and our endless imagination—to express the various realms in so many ways—until we become overwhelmed and confused with the sheer variety of understandings.

That may also be so.

A brief pause.

H. Let me narrow my focus. Originally I asked you the question: how am I? You have watched my unfoldings and my articulations. I really meant to ask you some more searching and personal questions. How have I done? And which direction should I go?

A. This you know yourself—more or less. You have not gone deep enough in your meditation. You have not succeeded in creating a deeper space for your continuous meditation. And somehow, you have not had enough courage to transcend further. Transcendence is an endless quest.

I know, I know. The normal circumstances of life are so jittery, so un-quiet, so un-peaceful. I have to escape to remote places, where I can find an external peace. Only then can I find the right circumstances to practice my deep meditation. One such place is

Greece and the village of Theologos, at the edge of which I am talking to you. Another such place are the Himalayan Hills where, in the midst of total tranquility and while surrounded by the grandeur of the Himalayas one can find new dimensions of one's existence.

But peace is ultimately the inner peace. You must find it inside yourself.

Yes, but external circumstances may help or may hamper and ultimately incapacitate you. It is not without a reason that the illustrious ones were escaping into the desert or some other places of seclusion—to arrive at the Great Peace.

Is transcendence also a matter of peace?

No, it is mainly the matter of courage, of getting out of yourself this inner substance, which is sitting there. I don't think I lack courage. But perhaps I don't have enough of it. This kind of courage, that is, which is piercing through all the walls, and, which is a bit mad. This touch of madness is exemplified by the Great Lights, which have succeeded. Our present times are characterized by the complete lack of courage. People are conditioned to be spineless

poodles, obedient ciphers, who only consume.

And you want to be burning with fire.

Yes, I don't want to be ordinary because it is a kiss of death, while one is alive. I want to be divinely mad. But not ordinarily mad. Ordinary madness has destroyed many inspired and ascending minds. I also want to be divinely lucid. For this kind of lucidity may be a vehicle of transcendence. What I find around myself is the sea of grayness. In this climate, transcendence is denied and sneered at.

But what prevents you to be transcendent in your personal life?

Actually nothing. Yet, one does not live and think in a vacuum. I do not say that I feel like a rat in a cage. I do my act of transcending. I tear apart the box in which they have tried to put me.

And so what is the problem? Where is the problem?

Well, yes, I see too many excellent and worthy minds, which have succumbed to the chains and "settled"—to live in a consumptive slavery. On another plane, I see too many great beings who were devoured by the flames and

44

perished—either being unjustly persecuted or by burning out within.

So what do you want to be? A Jesus? A Buddha? A Lao Tzu?

An interesting question. Do I dare to answer it? No, I don't want to be a Jesus. Among my brightest students, there were two who wanted to match Jesus—at different times, of course, not together. I watched their quest from excellence to divinity and then to madness until they found themselves in the lunatic asylum. I stood by them, carefully observing their painful decline and then their slow and wobbly recovery. The present Western culture claims to be derived from the teachings of Jesus. But it has become so confused by its amnesia that whoever claims to be an incarnation of Jesus is likely to be put behind bars.

It is hard to believe that. How strange is the dialectics of love— from sheer admiration to sheer exploitation. But what about the Buddha?

Well, he has not been persecuted by his own people. He did accomplish a wonderful peace and equanimity. He radiated this peace, just as much as Jesus' presence radiated love. Yet, there were three assassination attempts on his life.

He died rather tired at the age of 80—not by natural death actually; but by being inadvertently poisoned by mushrooms. He did not create any church. But he left behind 800 enlightened arhats.

It is not quite clear what you are trying to convey to me.

Perhaps that one cannot be a New Jesus, a New Buddha, a New Lao Tzu. They were the figures and the sources of energy uniquely exemplifying their times. We can only be their followers and the epigones.

This may be so. But still, the spiritual resources of humanity are enormous. You did not mention anything about Lao Tzu. Do you not find him admirable?

Yes, I do. He was such a free soul, so noble and benign and so beautifully enigmatic in the depth of his teaching. When his time was coming up, he somehow orchestrated his departure and his future. He was traveling on his yak—some say donkey—eastward, towards the great Tibetan planes. He knew that he could be stopped by the guard on the border. And he was. The guard recognized him— not by his misdemeanors but because of his wisdom — and told him that he could not cross the border unless he wrote up his teaching, his philosophy. Lao Tzu complied. For thirty days he was writing down his story, which became the immortal poem and philosophical treatise expressing the Taoist philosophy. His mission accomplished, he mounted his yak and went East—without any disciples or students accompanying him. Ultimately he became dissolved in the mist of the Himalayan Mountains. What a fitting end for such a peaceful and sublime philosopher.

It is a nice story. But tell me, are you a Taoist?

Well, no. But actually we are all Taoists, including you.

You have caught me off guard with your remark. Is Taoism such a deep philosophy that it includes even us, the stars?

And why not? Is it not deep and fathomless enough?

Another thoughtful pause. I felt that Annabel was about ready to close this dialogue.

A. Tell me, then, where you are with your own philosophy and your aspirations.

H. You tell me. I told you where I am not—yet.

I see. So you want me to help you.

You have already helped by listening to my peregrinations.

So where do we go from here?

You would say upward, to further transcendence.

I certainly would.

Transcendence is such a nice term; nay, such a powerful idea. You hold onto it and you are being carried forward and upward.

For you—is transcendence the end in itself, this divine process, which carries you furthered and further?

I hope not the end in itself but only an instrument, a vehicle, which will carry me to this land of bliss, within which, like Lao Tzu, I will be united with the Himalayan grandeur, light and all-knowing.

46

THE
7TH DIALOGUE

ON MEANING

At the beginning we returned to the previous dialogue and pondered over the question how is it that the stars need us humans for the articulation of their existence. Yes, we are thinking for the stars, but we are also part of the stars.

So who is thinking? Are the stars thinking through us? While we are thinking for them? Is it all self-referential? Are we just a mirror of self-reflecting lights? Is the whole universe an enormous hall of self-reflected light? Such was the beginning of our dialogue. And we immediately pushed the idea further: Is it all one stupendous tautology? The sameness of things under the mirage of glittering differences?

How is it possible that we are thinking for the stars and the stars are not thinking... but understand our thinking? And what do we understand by saying that: stars understand our thinking; or that they do not understand our thinking?

Pythagoras once exclaimed, "Astonishing! Everything is intelligent." And this insight was repeated in various formulations many times since; including contemporary physicists. But nobody dared to articulate this insight in any depth or length. As if everybody was afraid to tread where angels fear to enter. But the two of us, Annabel and myself, did not have such fears. Again, simultaneously, we ask each other: Is the Universe intelligent? And we burst with laughter of joy amidst a new comprehension.

We then returned to the idea of the self-referential nature of the Universe. What does it mean "the sameness of all things?" Now, even if they somewhat reflect each other in one stupendous hall of self-reference, are they the same? And what does it mean to say they are not the same?

We looked at each other bemused. Not confused, but rather looking with sympathy on the inadequacy of human language.

A. The humans are so proud and pompous that their language is so rich and versatile but they can't even say what it means that two things are the same or not the same.

H. It does not matter much whether two loaves of bread are the same or not the same; anyway, they will disappear soon by being eaten. But with cosmic matters, it makes the difference. Is all cosmos self-referential? Is the Universe intelligent?

Again, we smiled at each other when we considered these ideas, as if saying to each other: what does it matter? But we stopped smiling when the question pressed itself on us: what matters? What does matter? Is it again the language that is tripping and ensnaring us?

H. There are some philosophers who were aware of these accursed questions as they tried to grapple with the fundamental unity of the universe. One of them was the lonely Ludwig Wittgenstein, a mystic at heart, a rationalist by self-persuasion. He was cryptic in his utterances. The first proposition of the famous *Tractactus Logico-Philosophicus* asserts: "The world is everything that is the case."

A. One thinks that logicians are so clear in their thinking. But they can be quite obscure.

H. Correct, especially when they start thinking deep. Actually,

endless treatises were written on: what did Wittgenstein mean by his first proposition. I suppose he simply wanted to assert the fundamental unity of the Universe. But he couldn't. He didn't have a stellar companion, like Annabel, to engage him in dialogue.

A. If Wittgenstein had enough courage, he would have said: 'only the is Is.' Or simpler still: 'the is Is.'

H. This would be the most succinct ontology of the oneness of the Universe. It is astonishing that great things can be expressed so succinctly. Only that which exists exists; or the is Is.

At this moment a big shooting star crossed the horizon.

H. Right on, I said; all meaning is ephemeral.

A. How right you are.

We both reflected over the expression "all meaning is ephemeral." What does it mean exactly?

H. Isn't it so that language is but a web of words—a very fragile web for that matter. Can we demand of language to deliver us the Universe on a silver platter? How closely are we wedded to our language and to our mind? If we were divorced from language and the mind, then what? The end of the human race, the end of homo sapiens as we know it?

A. Probably so... (very slowly said Annabel. But she said it so slowly and ponderously as if it were not all she wanted to say.)

I look at her askance; she added:

A. Yes, there is more to the story, to what I would like to say, but there is no language for it, not in your kind of mind, not in your kind of reality.

She was speaking in riddles but I knew what she was hinting at. She was suggesting at that this point we are leaving behind the conventional human reality. And how could we talk about it while it was clearly beyond us. Annabel was reading my mind and nodded slightly. Then there was a long silence between us. Finally I gropingly said:

H. You are talking or hinting at the multiplicity of realities, which some philosophers and even dramatists postulated.

A. Yes... (she responded, but again with some reluctance.)

H. I know the problem: how can we talk about these things if we can't? The same Wittgenstein said that what can't be talked about we should consign to silence.

A. Correct.

But human beings have notoriously talked about things, which cannot be expressed in the accepted human language. Some of these things were impossible for the human mind to accept. Some were simply crazy or mad.

The impossible you can try. Individual human beings and humanity as a whole, tried the impossible many times—only to enlarge their domains and the scope of their being. But to attempt what is simply crazy is another matter...

...and she stopped here. And I wondered why. Hmmm. Was she warning me personally—not to go too far, so... that I do not get locked in a lunatic asylum? I was touched by her personal concern. She read my thoughts.

A. Yes, I am concerned. Well. You probably have got about 30,000 days to live on this planet. Each of them is difficult as it is. Why end your remaining days locked up as insane?

H. (Now I laughed at her). Is it from you that I hear such words?

Isn't it so that one day lived in glory, in the resplendent lucidity of the stellar light, is worthy 10,000 of dreary ordinary days? Besides, who is insane on this planet? Those who wage imperial wars and are killing people by hundred of thousands? Or the stargazers, who try to see more lucidly for the benefit of all?

A. How right you are! But the seers, who see clearly and perspicuously, must not be mowed down before their time.

The remaining time we spent in a non-verbal communication. It was a kind of telepathic exchange. There were many ideas we were exchanging, but rather tentatively and gropingly. We were musing what would it be like, for a human being, to enter the sphere of an alternative reality. Would we need to lose our identity in the process? Are there some beings in this universe that can dwell in the multiplicity of realities? Can God do that? If so, what kind of entity is s/he while being in different realities? We did not try to draw any conclusions. For how can

you?—while your mind is imprisoned by the present condition of the human species?

But I didn't want to end this dialogue with silence.

H. How are we going to resolve our problems? Where is evolution leading us?

A. The universe is immense. You are still in the infancy of your understanding. You are still unable to govern yourself because you are deficient in understanding. You talk about the explosion of knowledge during the last century. But your understanding, and your knowledge of yourself are still puny. You will become bigger. You will become great. Your universe then will become great. Your practical and existential problems will be resolved.

Will we be happy then?

That is another matter. (And she added impatiently)… When you are spiritually fulfilled you don't need to be happy.

THE
8TH DIALOGUE

WHAT ARE
THE STARS FOR?

The night is very warm. I spread my canvas on the appointed spot in the mountains. A brief shooting star welcomes me at the beginning. All is well. As usual, the dialogue is very slow to start. My mind is meandering among the stars with no purpose at all. Well, the presence of the stars is purpose enough. Bits of dialogue start to develop with Annabel but without much coherence. We muse how the people on Earth can be helped.

A. They can't be helped because they don't want to be helped.

H. Yet, they do because they know that they are stuck in so many ways.

Yes, there are all kinds of knots and paradoxes on the way. Their wants are not what they need. Their wants are in the way of their needs.

And here is another problem: how can we impose on the people the needs they need in spite of their wants to the contrary?

Isn't it what you do with small children? You subtly graft on them the needs, which will serve them well in the long run, while ignoring and suppressing their wants and whims of the moment.

So should we conclude that at present the unseeing humanity is a bunch of children? This problem of wants and needs is, in a sense so flimsy, and yet so important. So often wants and needs are interwoven in the same tapestry of living. So wants are part of our needs.

It is not how we should look at them. In the historical evolution of man, primitive wants are gradually transcended in favor of more refined and sublime needs.

So you are suggesting that needs are related to the higher tiers of human life while wants and urges to the lower ones?

The division is not so neat and clear. The needs for shelter and food, and also for security, are real ones. But the problem we are confronting in present times is a strange devolution of the human agenda: more refined and versatile needs are squeezed out in favor of more primitive consumptive wants.

I suppose that you want to say that consumptive wants have created the consumptive consciousness, which does not want to hear about any higher needs and aspirations. Thus you cannot convince people about their real needs if and when they are so blinded by the consumer wants? The paradox is that there is the freedom to satisfy the wants but... not the freedom to satisfy genuine needs. And even stars cannot help us in this matter.

I would not be so rushed about the stars. In any case, this is not what the stars are supposed to be doing. I hope and trust you would agree with me. Let us start with you. Could you tell me directly, as far as you are concerned: What are the stars for?

H. You are putting me on the spot. But... OK, why do I gaze at the stars and dialogue with them? What are they for?

- to give me the sense of space and of the infinity of the universe...
- to give me the peace within which is vast and endless...
- to give me the breadth and depth of life unparalleled by any other source...

- to give me the sense of beauty and radiance of the Cosmos not to be found elsewhere.

H. Well, to put it simply, the stars are for augmenting everything which is great in me.

A. I am pleased you could put it so well.

Then we went into an altogether different direction. At first we mused at the question of the human mind and human consciousness. Surely, we decided, there must be one common human mind embracing all humanity, all human species. But in addition, or perhaps on the top of it, there are so many different human consciousnesses. Each epoch seems to have a different consciousness; and perhaps each human being possesses a different consciousness. What a bewildering variety!

While we were contemplating human consciousness, a question flickered through my mind, which I expressed loudly to Annabel.

H. What about the mind of the universe?

A. What about it? (Annabel was a bit alarmed.)

Can we explore it a bit?

(Annabel was clearly unnerved at this point). No, we can't. I can't do it.

Why so?

Because to grasp the mind of the universe, you have to be outside of it, looking at it from a vantage point of a more superior universe. We can't do it.

I was not so alarmed at the prospect as Annabel was, and said:

H. Perhaps there is one agency within this universe which can do that.

A. Which one is that?

H. The human mind… perhaps this is a great god of the universe… the agency, which can look at the universe outside itself and also at itself—at the same time.

Annabel was rather perplexed on this occasion. There was a long, long silence between us. I decided to return to the village. There are some dialogues which have clear conclusions, and some which are disturbingly open. I bid goodbye to Annabel and to the theatre of the stars. I was not disappointed on the way back. Rather I was intrigued with the possibility of exploring this enthralling subject—the mind of the universe.

THE
9TH DIALOGUE

ON
GREAT FREEDOM

The kaleidoscope of stars is surrounding me on all sides. They are dancing around in a strange somnambulistic way. How can there be so much radiance in one place? I am again lying down on the ground looking at Annabel, which shines just above me. Only the crickets are singing, otherwise a beautiful silence. I am musing to myself whether I should return to this great subject: the mind of the universe. A thought flickers through my mind: who am I to even touch such a subject, while my mind is so puny that I cannot understand who I am? Then I smile to myself thinking, "Have the great prophets understood who they were? I doubt it. If they did, they probably would have never entered the thorny path of enlightening of others." Annabel is watching my ruminations from a distance. But she does not say anything. "Who am I?" I ask myself explicitly. And "where am I?" Now Annabel subtly enters the discourse.

A. You are where you are, comfortably lying on your canvas.

H. Well, it is not such a great revelation to be told that.

A. Perhaps it is, if you think about it deeper.

So I think about it deeper. Yes, there is this enormous sense of peace around me and within me; and also this great sense of freedom.

A. Enjoy this sense of freedom. Just enjoy being here as you are. Forget your continuous ruminations how to justify this and that; how to make your knowledge deeper and more coherent. There is no need for that.

H. What do you mean? I must know in order to be.

Perhaps not so. To be as you are is sufficient.

It can't be. I must know — even that I am here…

You see you are again disturbing your tranquility and your beautiful freedom with your ceaseless and often useless inquiry. Yes, you can just be within the fold of freedom and peace — without thinking and ruminating.

I have followed her advice. The sense of my well-being is simply all pervading. I am trying not to think. But I observe the state of my being. Why is this freedom so all embracing and profound — in the theatre of stars and not elsewhere — I do not know. But I know the feeling of it. I am one with the stars. Not completely dissolving into their stellar substance but being completely wrapped by their presence. Why this freedom and peace? Because all earthly matters pale in significance. ALL—the trivial and the so-called important.

The Theatre of the Stars is one and only. If you spend in it some time, you understand what it is all about, or at least are beginning to understand. We, humans, are all gazing at the stars from time to time — but most of the time mindlessly. How can we be so torpid and un-seeing? Is it because we are thinking too much? No, it can't be so. It is the wrong kind of thinking that alienates us from ourselves, from nature and the stars.

Now I realize that I have been ruminating myself. So I am trying to bring myself back to the pristine state of only BEING, while enjoying this enormous freedom of my state of being. In a subtle subconscious way, my mind has been trying to answer the questions: "How is this peaceful state of being important to our well-being? Why do we ruin our peaceful well-being with continuous rushing and half-baked and often aggressive thinking"?

Annabel has been smiling in the background and was not commenting. She knew that I was experiencing one of the most important hours of my life. And she also knew that I might not be able to share it with anybody on Earth. The solitude of a lonely stargazer? Not quite that, but the sense that you are learning something so beautiful and profound that your heart and mind are singing with delight. Yet you also feel sadness because you might not be able to share what the stars have told you.

A couple of days later, I asked myself what was the most important thing that I learnt on this evening of Great Freedom among the stars? As I looked again and again over the starry constellation, the overwhelming feeling was that the universe is AFFIRMATION, that being itself is affirmation, that life is affirmation. It was so clear to me that the universe and existence (including human) is affirmation. No ifs and buts, no stutters and stammers — only one splendid continuous affirmation. It was so easy to accept this affirmation while gazing at the stars.

Why then, I asked myself, has human thought made everything so twisted, problematic, doubtful, cynical and skeptical? Why are so many philosophies gloomy, grim, pessimistic, cynical and nihilistic? My answer was that people, and philosophers especially, do not spend enough time with the stars and do not seriously look at them. They don't understand that right philosophy, good philosophy, even half decent philosophy is one of affirmation; and so must be our life. Affirmation is a condition for living.

THE
10TH DIALOGUE

WITH THE STARS

I am again in the mountains for my dialogues with the stars. After a prolonged silence, I start my dialogue with the supplication:

Oh, loving sisters
Keep me crazy
But not insane.
Insanity must be avoided
For it is a catastrophe.
Craziness is an elevated
State of imagination.
It must be cultivated.

Then there is a long silence. And finally I hear the whispers of Annabel:

A. In the future you will all be transformed.

H. The whole of humanity?

A. Yes.

I am musing to myself on the meaning of the term "trans-form." It is deeper than re-form or de-form, but it is distinctly less than being transmogrified or transmuted.

In a flash of imagination, I SEE humanity so transformed that we are changed beyond recognition — all our problems and dilemmas are gone; but also our emotions, loves, inspiringly written poems — and yes — our quest for transcendence.

Would that be worth it? To be SO transformed… I am thinking to myself. I can see that Annabel is watching the permutations of my mind with a derisive smile. She says nothing. But her smile tells me: "You have always wanted to transcend all stations, all obstacles, dilemmas and trivial problems."

I want to protest a little and say: I know, I know… But her derisive smile is paralyzing. Beyond this derisive smile, there is another one, more divine, hiding. And this one asks me: "How much humanity do you want to claim? And how much divinity? What if there is a trade off between the two?"

I understand the question. But I don't really want to answer it. In a flash I answer it to myself and to her: "The existence of a true mystic is a most sublime form of human existence." And then Annabel confronts me with another cutting question: "And how much humanity will be then left in you?"

I try to ignore this question as well. Am I afraid of far-reaching questions? Or is she just cutting me too much tonight, forgetting that I am human, thus vulnerable?

Blue Tara, her sister nearby, tells me: "Your problems will be resolved. YOU HAVE, IN FACT, NO PROBLEMS AT ALL."

Reassuringly she adds: "Look at the intensity of the radiance in this triangle. It is yours for the keeping! Whenever you are in any need, come back to the glory of this radiance. Everything else is vanitas vanitatis."

I look at the whole firmament around me.

The stars are so immensely radiant tonight.

I am so intoxicated and inspired by them.

I feel so lucky to be alive tonight.

Smilingly, I return to the village.

EPILOGUE:

HOW HAVE I LEARNT TO DIALOGUE WITH STARS?

Stars are so far away, so radiant and so far beyond us. The Earth is so sullen, so rudimentary and so immediate. Can an earthling like me possess the stars? Yes, through this incredible magic that resides in the universe.

Nothing happens in this universe without the mind being a part of it, really being a choreographer of it. This cosmos is a strange tale, in which stars and humans, the whales and nightingales all participate, most of the time in joy and sometimes amidst suffering.

If your mind is entirely fixed on the earth and if you see in the earth nothing but dust, you are not great news for the universe. One speck of dust is the same as all others. However, one human being is never the same as any other human being. When human beings begin to converse with the stars, cosmic stories are being acted out.

Let us remember: to become a human being is a difficult act; and it is also a great privilege. To learn the language of art and of poetry, in which the whisperings of stars are often expressed is not a work for toddlers. Human knowledge and crafts are stupendous in their scope and depth. But dialoguing with stars is quite another story. Actually, an exquisite story.

I have gone to various schools. I studied music, engineering and philosophy. Oxford University was kind enough to accommodate me for a number of years and provide me with what is considered superior education. How did it help me to converse with the stars? Not at all! I had to unlearn Oxford to be able to converse with the stars. How does one unlearn Oxford? Is it allowed? Are you not then considered a renegade? Well, perhaps a little. But when you are on a stellar track, you are not bothered by the opinions of pedantic scholars. Especially when you are submerging yourself in the magma of the cosmos.

How do you begin to dialogue with stars? There is no beginning. It just happens. How did it happen to me? Slowly. I first had to acquire a large perspective on all manner of things. Understanding the world in conventional terms is not sufficient for dialoguing with the stars. You need to enlarge your perspective on the entire cosmos in which stars are given prominence. You need to develop this enormous largeness of mind in which you can comprehend that you are made of stellar dust, and that all is one, and that stars are part of your being. At first it may be a bit difficult. But after a while you get used to it. My path has also included enlarging the boundaries of my culture. Every culture is muzzling us and it tries to condition us. But you and I are stellar beings. We cannot be country bumpkins for our entire life.

I have been always aware that other people—in their cultures—are made of the same cosmic stuff as we are. Thus I studied Upanishads of the Hindu culture. One of these Upanishads claims that Joy is primary and it had existed before gods. I studied Taoism and was impressed by the fluidity of the Taoist thinking. In one of his discourses, Lau Tzu maintains that the road, which can be defined, is not the right road; the right road cannot be defined.

Art has always fascinated me as an extraordinary expression of human genius. The energy contained in works of art has been dazzling to me. And so was the light emanating from art—a form of magic.

When I finished writing my major Eco-philosophy books, I became an "artist," of sort, sculpting large pieces in white marble. My first assignment in philosophy of art was a series of seminars, at the Academy of Fine Arts in Helsinki, in Finland. In one of the seminars, I was prompted to say that all sculpture is light, and furthermore, that all art is light. That created some consternation. But only for awhile.

My continuous interaction with art and creativity enabled me later to understand in depth this enormous spectacle, which the universe of stars is offering us. The Theatre of the Stars is amazing. And the stars, the main actors, are both so unbelievable and so natural. He who has watched this theatre, while deeply submerged in the cosmic substance, is both awed and nourished by the cosmic energy of the stars. In some Tibetan Buddhist texts it is claimed that we can eat energy of the stars directly during the night. But it requires some special skills.

Light is the source of all existence. But also the foundation of our ethical spine. Altruism is not a human invention. It is an essential vehicle through which the universe unfolds.

In addition to intellectual and spiritual preparations, my dialogues with the stars required more physical preparations—especially in choosing right locations for viewing the stars. I needed to find for myself right hills and mountains. Among many, two locations turned out to be my favorite. The first ware the hills in the Himalayas, in Tehri Garhwal region, near the village called Ranichauri. A most satisfying place. Complete darkness, great luminosity and radiance of stars. And the sense that I was embraced by the Himalayas. This was an experience that was thrilling to the bones. Yet, there was a little drawback. I was in the midst of wild Himalayas, where panthers occasionally roamed. And I was told to be "cautious." I wish they had not told me about the panthers.

Thus the village of Theologos, on the island of Thassos in Greece, became my main theatre of the stars for dialoguing with my stellar sisters. I knew this island for many years. Thassos is a mountainous island. It does not have high mountains but it possesses wild mountains.

My initiation to full dialogues with the star that I called Annabel was slow. I first walked through wild paths of the island, as high as possible, toward the main peak of mount Ipsarion. The hike would take 5 hours up the mountain and 5 hours down the mountain. Then I discovered parts of the island quite secluded and relatively close to my village (some 20-30 minutes walking). No panthers or even snakes but only goats and sheep. I found my favorite terraces from which I could gaze at my favorite constellations, while I was laying on the grass. I was thrilled.

So I was gazing on moonless nights more and more often; at time, being completely entranced by the interpenetrating radiance of the stars. I would occasionally mutter to myself and to the stars: "Who am I?" "Who are you?"… as if asking for help. At that time I thought they could not hear me. Then I became somewhat acquainted with their energy and the sense of their being. Then half playfully, I started to imagine that they could hear me and I CAN HEAR THEM. It was a slow process, based on the conviction that since I was a stellar being, made ultimately of the stellar dust, I should be able to discourse with radiant beings of the heavens.

Thus various dialogues started to emerge, haltingly but surely. These first, half-coherent dialogues, I was able to articulate in a recognizable human language. And then present them under the title: Dialogues with the Stars. The main star of my conversations, as I already mentioned, is Annabel.

73

What is hers and what is mine in the dialogues will require the superior judgment of the reader. It is actually up to each of us to determine what bits of knowledge are worthy of our attention and which are not. Deep and new knowledge is so often rejected because of the lack of imagination of shallow people.

We must be truly open to the magic of the cosmos, and of the stars, to be able to truly appreciate who we are and what it is all about.

Those who embrace the stars, in whatever way they can, are privileged rays of stellar beauty. Those are able to dialogue with the stars are shaping the meaning of the universe.

HYMN TO LIGHT

1.

O Light, eternal Light
How beautiful you are!
Your everlasting beauty has enabled us
To create things in the image of beauty.
All the images we conceive and bring to reality
Are but a reflection of your celestial designs.
Our minds and hands are capable and dexterous.
They are like a loom weaving endless patterns.
But you are the Loomer behind the loom.

2.

For the miracles of your infinite powers
We thank you, O Light.
In your presence life opens up, matures and blossoms.
In your absence, life withers, decays and dies.
A slender blade of grass is capable
Of piercing through a surface of asphalt
By following your call to arise to light.
A delicate flower of the apple tree
Becomes a succulent apple.
By your hidden guidance, a little chick in the egg
Breaks through its shell
And emerges to freedom, movement and joy.
We do not understand your miraculous powers
But we do appreciate their fruit and sustenance.
O Light, you are a giver of such excellences.

3.

O Light, you are so kind and ingenious.
You created the seed in men
To be gently planted in the Mother's womb.
You continued your generosity while overseeing the seed
To become a small child, then a growing being.
Then this growing being begins to speak coherently.
And then he writes verses
Inspired by your luminosity and radiance.
What a miracle to create the human seed.
What a miracle when this seed finally writes poems.
There are no limits to your miracles.
We are enthralled by your great theatre of magic.

4.

We thank you, O Light, for teaching us by your own example.
Being as generous as you are
You are teaching us generosity.
Being as altruistic as you are
You are teaching us altruism.
Being so benign and even-handed to all beings
You are teaching us compassion and justice.
You are such a splendid and generous Mother!
We have resolved to follow you
In loving the whole creation.
We do not need any book of ethics.
You are this book!
In so far as we understand your compassion and generosity,
In so far as we are your children and continuators,
We are obliged to follow your altruism and solidarity.

5.

How is it possible that works of art
Contain so much light in them?
It is amazing that human beings can put
So much luminous light is in their works of art.
The whole scene of art and of knowledge
Are little lamps illuminating all our horizons.
If all these lamps were blown out
Then there would be deep darkness.
And this darkness would simply mean
The death of the soul.
You are part of our essential soul, O Light.
Oh, how exciting it is to live in the universe of Light,
In which art can be so luminous,
And knowledge can shine and illumine.

6.

O Light, you are the source of all Divinity.
Other divine beings, gods and deities
Derive their substance and meaning
From the core of your being.
No god or religion can aspire to be divine
If it does not claim to be of light.
By exalting light as the most important spiritual substance,
All religions, churches, creeds, and spiritual movements
Are simply paying homage to you as spiritually supreme.
Everything is divine, yes, because everything derives from you.
The whole world basks in divinity
Because it bathes in your light.

41061371R00049

Made in the USA
Lexington, KY
01 May 2015